Organic Art Emporium
A meditative tool for all ages

Dark Attic Publishing is located in Indiana. This book was illustrated, designed, and written by Lori Geisler. Published by Dark Attic Publishing. The copyright belongs to Dark Attic Publishing as of 2016. We reserve all of our rights. Printing in the United States of America.

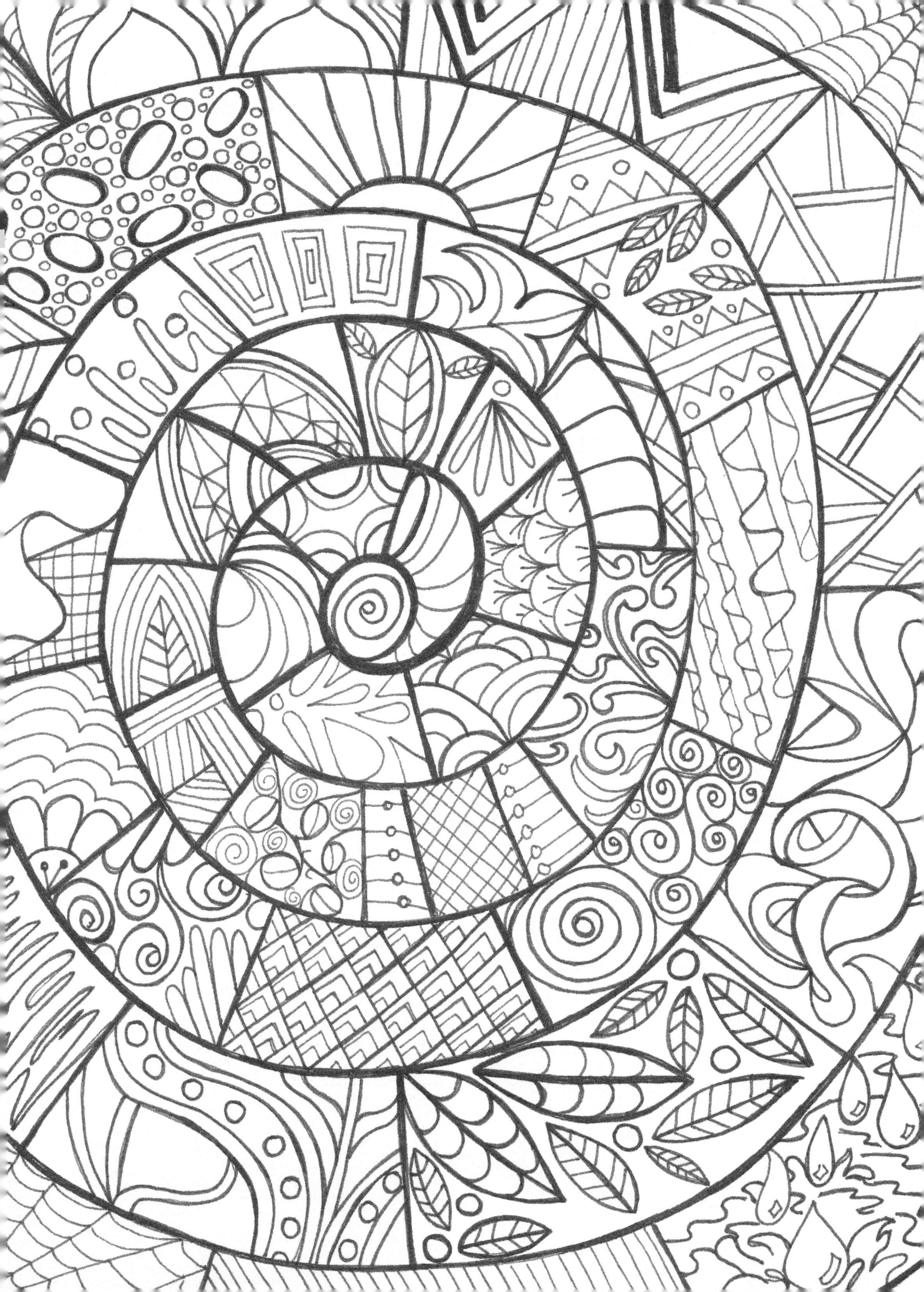

Available @ Amazon, Barnes and Noble and Blue Star websites

Doodle Emporium

A Stress Relieving Adult Coloring Book

Lori Geisler

Blue Star

Connect with Lori Geisler:

https://www.facebook.com/LoriGeisler-250165104996463/

https://www.pinterest.com/kayageisler/

https://twitter.com/LoriKayaGeisler

Kayageisler@yahoo.com

www.ingramcontent.com/pod-product-compliance
Lightning Source LLC
Chambersburg PA
CBHW081221020426
42331CB00012B/3064